With thanks to Leen Decin, professor of astronomy,
and Kitty Peeters, teacher

Copyright © 2022 Clavis Publishing Inc., New York

Originally published as *De sterrenkundige* in Belgium and the Netherlands by Clavis Uitgeverij, 2021
English translation from the Dutch by Clavis Publishing Inc., New York

Visit us on the Web at www.clavis-publishing.com.

Astronomers and What They Do written and illustrated by Liesbet Slegers

ISBN 978-1-60537-741-4

This book was printed in October 2021 at Nikara, M. R. Štefánika 858/25, 963 01 Krupina, Slovakia.

First Edition
10 9 8 7 6 5 4 3 2 1

Astronomers
and What They Do
Liesbet Slegers

Clavis

NEW YORK

*We humans live
on planet Earth*

At night, when it's dark and there are few clouds,

the moon and the stars appear in the sky.

How beautiful! But what else is up there that we can't see?

Using special instruments, astronomers can tell us lots about the sun,

the moon, and the other planets up there in space.

Astronomers often work at night so they can see the stars
and planets well. Sometimes they travel to the mountains,
where they can see the sky even more clearly.
This astronomer is dressed for the cold mountain air and
is wearing a cozy hat, thick gloves, sturdy pants, and warm shoes.

During the day, astronomers wear **sunglasses** to protect their eyes against the bright sun.

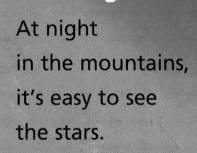

At night
in the mountains,
it's easy to see
the stars.

In the thin mountain air,
an **oxygen bottle** helps
the astronomer breathe.

Computers receive information from telescopes.

Astronomers work in a special building called an **observatory**.
In the dome at the top is a **telescope**. It works like binoculars
but is much, much stronger. Sometimes the astronomer uses
a **yellow laser beam** to help see the stars and planets more clearly.
There are many types of telescopes, even telescopes that float around in space.

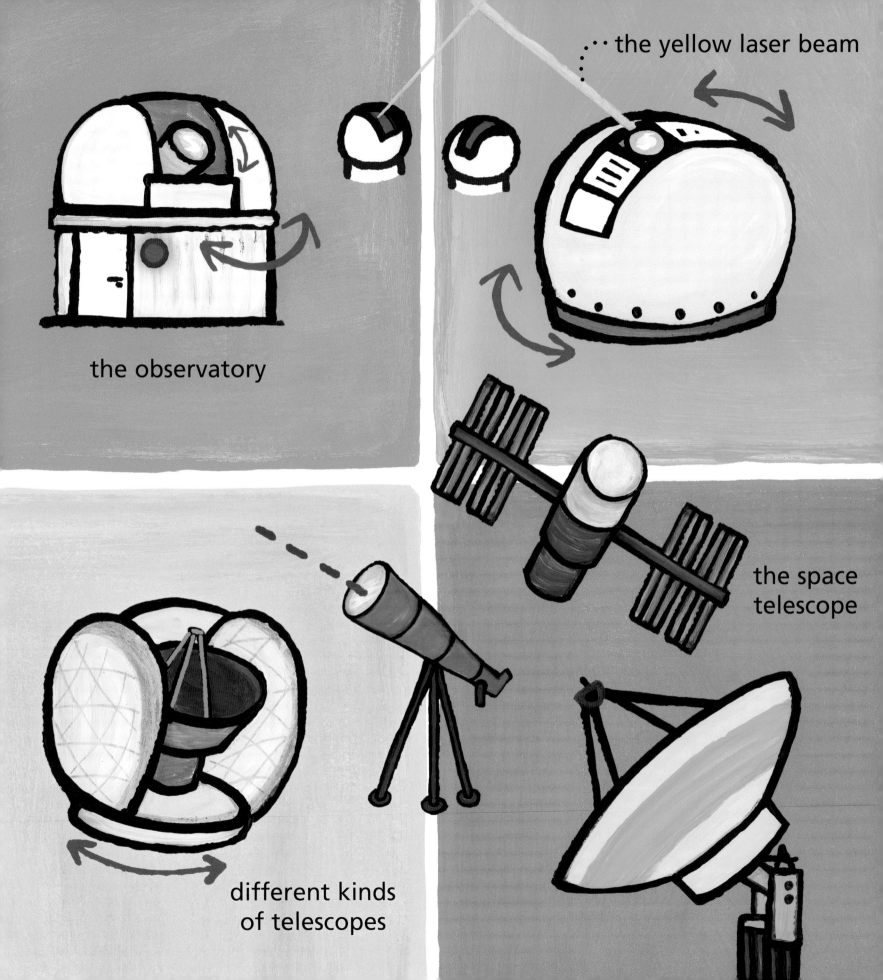

the observatory

the yellow laser beam

the space telescope

different kinds of telescopes

*In the daytime, the shutter
on the dome is closed,
but at night, it opens and
the telescope comes out.
The whole dome can rotate.
Cool!*

This is the observatory, where the astronomer looks through
the telescope and works on her computers. During the day,
the shutter closes to protect the telescope from rain, dirt,
or bird droppings. When it's clear at night, with no clouds
in sight, the dome opens and the telescope comes out.
The astronomer aims it and looks up high in the starry sky.
What will she see tonight?

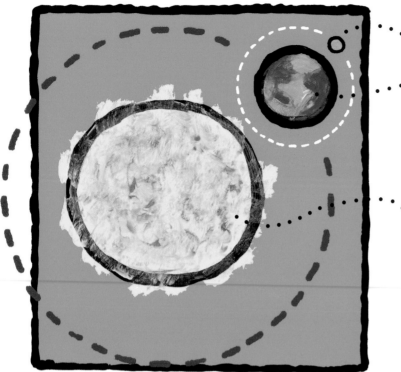 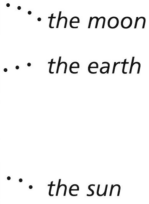

the moon

the earth

the sun

The astronomer adjusts the telescope throughout the night
to follow the moon and the stars as they move across the night sky.
Even though we can't feel it, the earth is spinning all the time.
It's also rotating around the sun. And the moon is rotating
around planet Earth! The stars move too, but we can't see that
because they're so far away. How crazy is that?

It's dark and quiet outside.
The astronomer has to be very patient,
because research can take a long time.

The astronomer packs her suitcase. Tomorrow, she leaves for another observatory in a distant country. She's going to the high mountains to study a large group of stars. From a very high place, she can see many more stars in the sky. And she sees them much more clearly there, too. In her suitcase, she puts nice warm clothes. She mustn't forget her long, warm tights and her gloves.

In the mountains are big, fantastic telescopes. How do they work?
To look at a star, the astronomer points the telescope at it.
The light from the star falls on a large mirror in the telescope
and bounces up to a smaller mirror, which sends the information
to a measuring instrument at the bottom. The information then
goes to the astronomer's computers. By capturing the rays of light,
the astronomer can study space.

the small mirror

The light from the star falls into the large, hollow mirror of the telescope.

the measuring instrument

We can see all the colors of a rainbow with our eyes: red, orange, yellow, green, blue, indigo, and violet.

What exactly is light? Light is made of waves of energy.

When the waves are close together, they make one color (purple!).

When they're far apart, they make a different color (red!).

If the waves of energy are too close or too far apart, we can't see the light with our eyes. But with different kinds of telescopes, the astronomer can capture all of the light from a star and study it.

the light

We can't see this piece of light with our eyes.

Our eyes can only see the visible light: the colors of the rainbow.

We can't see this piece of light with our eyes.

Some telescopes work during the day, when the sun is shining and even when it's cloudy.

After a busy night, the astronomer is getting some sleep.
The sun is shining, so the shutters of her observatory
are closed. Sleep tight, astronomer!
We'll see you later, when we can see the stars again.

In the city, it's hard to see the sky clearly because of the many lights.

In the evening, the astronomer wakes up.

She's eager to get back to work. The sun is setting,

and if you look closely, you can see the moon shining softly.

In the city, it's hard to see the stars because of all the lights.

This is called light pollution. But in the mountains,

where it's incredibly dark, it's much easier to see the night sky.

The star twinkles as it moves across the sky.

When the astronomers sit in their observatories, they aim the telescopes at the place in space they want to study. They do this with a special kind of GPS, kind of like the GPS that helps you find your way in a car. The yellow laser beams also help guide them through the night sky. The telescopes and the domes rotate all night long, so the astronomers can follow the stars and planets as they move across the sky.

By working together, astronomers all over the world make fun and interesting discoveries.

On her many computers, the astronomer gets to work
on the information that has come in from the telescope.
She also consults with other astronomers all over the world.
If she has learned something new about the night sky, she's delighted!

What have astronomers discovered?
Quite a lot!

Facts about the sun, the earth, and other planets

The most famous star is . . . the sun! It's a star that shines during the day.
Planet Earth revolves around the sun, and there are other planets that
revolve around the sun too. Do you see them?

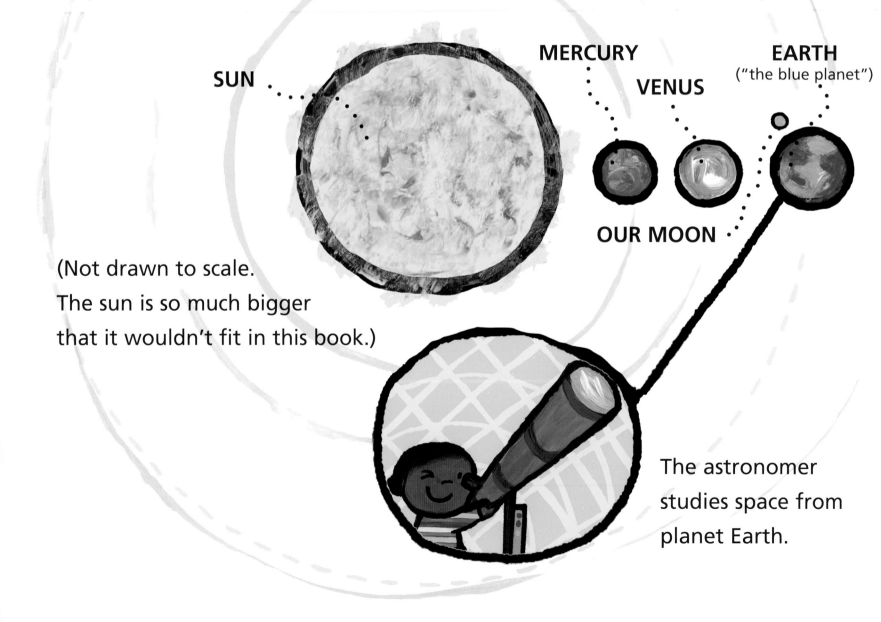

SUN

MERCURY

VENUS

EARTH
("the blue planet")

OUR MOON

(Not drawn to scale.
The sun is so much bigger
that it wouldn't fit in this book.)

The astronomer
studies space from
planet Earth.

There are many moons in space. They all revolve around their planet, so our moon rotates around planet Earth. We can see our moon in the sky at night and sometimes during the day.

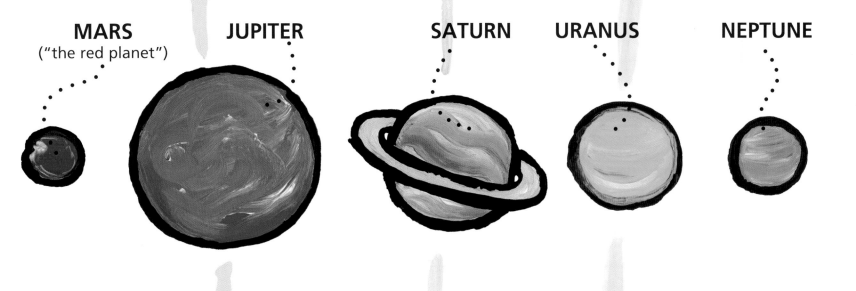

MARS
("the red planet")

JUPITER

SATURN

URANUS

NEPTUNE

Because of all that rotating, the earth sometimes comes directly between the moon and the sun. That's called an **eclipse**. When that happens, you can see the earth's shadow move across the moon.

Facts about stars

We all know about yellow stars. But did you know that there are blue stars and red stars as well? It's only the yellow ones that you can easily see with your eyes at night (and they're really white, if you look closely). But the telescope can see them all just fine!

Blue stars are super-hot. Yellow ones and red ones aren't as hot. Just look at a real flame. (Not for too long, because that's bad for your eyes.) The hottest part of a flame is also blue.

How do you draw a real star? We often draw stars with points. But a real star doesn't actually look like that. It's a round fireball, like our sun.

Each star is a shiny ball of
burning gas. Because of all
that glowing and burning,
we can see the stars in
the sky at night. Wow!

A star is born, lives,
and burns out.

Now, you might be wondering:
will our sun ever burn out?
Yes, but not for a very, very long
time from now.

When you see a shooting star,
you get to make a wish. But actually
that flash of light isn't a star at all.
It's a rock or a speck of dust
called a **meteor**.

The star we know best is our sun.
We only see the sun during the day,
but it's always there.

The Milky Way

Planet Earth is in
one of the spirals
of the Milky Way.

A galaxy is a large group of stars
that belong together. Our sun is
a star in the Milky Way Galaxy, and
planet Earth is part of the Milky Way too.
The Milky Way is a large, flat spinning disk.
From space, it looks like the spiral of a snail
shell, but from Earth we can only see it
from its side. It looks a bit like spilled milk.
That's how it got its funny name!

Your turn!

1 **Find** the moon in the sky when it's dark. Then look for the moon sometime later. Did you notice that the moon is not in the same place? That's because the earth and the moon are always rotating.

2 Now take a **look** at the moon with binoculars. Do you see the lines and spots? Those are mountains and holes on the moon's surface!

Food for thought

What's the difference between an **astronomer** and an **astronaut**?

An astronomer stays here on Earth, to explore space with telescopes. An astronaut travels to space.

The space telescope has discovered a new planet!
The planet is orbiting its star.

the star

the new planet

the space telescope

Create your own planet!

The space telescope flies into space
to take pictures of the stars and planets.
Sometimes a new planet is discovered. Maybe
it's covered with water, with crazy fish and water
monsters swimming around. What do you think is
out there? Draw a picture of a new planet, with new
creatures. Then come up with a fun name for your planet!

How good is your stargazing?

The sun sets in the west.

These drawings show the sun in the morning, the afternoon, and the evening—but they're out of order! Can you point to what happens first? What happens next? What happens last?

The sun rises in the east.

The sun is at her highest in the south.

And did you know this? The sun is never in the north!